D1000094

DATE DUE

2·24 12			

Demco, Inc. 38-293

PLAN OF THE CITY OF NEW YORK.

A Negro History Tour of Manhattan

by

M. A. ("Spike") Harris

Greenwood Publishing Corporation
New York

Harris, M. A., 1908-
A Negro history tour of Manhattan, by M. A.
"Spike" Harris.
F128.9.N3 H35 1968

RSN=00003148

Library of Congress catalog card number: 68-54217

Greenwood Publishing Corporation
211 East 43rd Street, New York, N. Y. 10017

Printed in the United States of America

Acknowledgments

The author and publisher gratefully acknowledge the use of photographs and illustrations supplied or prepared for this book by the following organizations and individuals:

The Home Insurance Company; the Institute for Historical Studies of Brooklyn; Sam Heyward and Casco Williams of the New Amsterdam Musical Association, Inc.; Negro History Associates; Julian McBrowne; and Werner J. Kuhn. Their generous cooperation has been invaluable in helping to prepare this book for publication.

The endpapers contain a surveyors plan of the City of New York (1803), reproduced through the courtesy of the New-York Historical Society.

CONTENTS

Part Two—City Hall

Part Three—Greenwich Village

Part Seven—Central Park

Part Eight—Harlem

M. A. Harris

ABOUT THE AUTHOR

M. A. HARRIS likes to say that no one but his mother knows his first name. He has been called "Spike" since his boyhood days in Brooklyn, New York, where he earned his nickname in athletics. He tried to drop out of high school, but his father and the truant officer caught him—a situation for which he is eternally grateful. Between basketball and tennis with varsity teams at Howard University, he earned a bachelor of arts degree in sociology. Thirty-four years later, he received a master of social work degree from Fordham University. In between degrees, he worked with Boys' Clubs and the Y.M.C.A. During World War II he served as a Red Cross Field Director in the Southwest Pacific. Most of the intervening years since his graduation from Howard have been spent in working with adult delinquents.

"Spike" Harris' career as a Negro history detective began when he did research to trace his paternal ancestors through the slavery period in the United States back to 1761. He found cause for so much pride in his family, and in the American Negro in general, that he continued the research as a hobby. The results of his digging into the past are shared in the form of filmstrips in schools from coast to coast and in an exhibit on Negro history used for teacher training. He describes his personal collection of rare books, documents and artifacts as "fair to middling."

INTRODUCTION

NEW YORK CITY is made up of five boroughs—Manhattan, Brooklyn, Queens, the Bronx and Staten Island—but to many people, including the author, New York means Manhattan. It was this small island (about thirteen miles long and two miles wide) that the early Dutch settlers bought from the Indians for $24 worth of beads and trinkets. Since the early 1600's, people from every country on earth have come here, bringing their languages and customs and blending in with those who came before. Many of these were Negroes, but a stroll along Manhattan streets reveals almost nothing except dark faces to connect Negroes with the history of New York City. That is what this book is all about. It will try to bring back to life some streets, neighborhoods, events and people that helped to make Manhattan what it is today.

This book does not pretend to be a Negro history textbook. Some historical material is added to the descriptions of locations simply to show the significance of certain places. This guide is designed to add a new dimension to sightseeing trips in Manhattan. If it should also lead to a more thorough study of the American Negro, the student is sure to benefit.

On reading references to slavery in early New York, remember this: not every Negro who came to America was a slave, nor was every white person free. Somewhere in the background of many Americans there is probably a slave ancestor. Unfortunately, slavery is as old as mankind and it still exists in some backward regions of the world. It is not what our ancestors were that is important; it's learning the lessons contained in history. These lessons, once learned, can prevent the repetition of the same old mistakes.

The history of the Negro in America is one of the world's all-time great dramas. Each of us plays a part and the end is not yet in sight. Let this Negro History Tour be a giant stride towards a happy ending.

STREET MAP OF
LOWER MANHATTAN

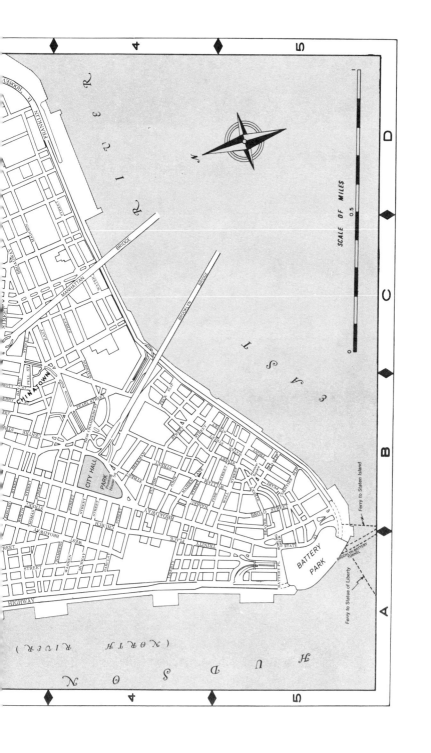

Commemorative plaque showing a scale model ground plan of Fort George. The plaque is located at 1 Bowling Green.

PART ONE

IN OLD NEW YORK

THE FIRST settlement on Manhattan Island was in the area now known as the financial district, at the southern tip of the island. The excellent natural harbor provided a place for the ships to land, and since there were no roads to carry people and goods further inland—indeed, there was nothing to travel to—the settlers built their first houses right along the shore. As time passed, and more people came, the settlement spread further north and east. And that original settlement is still growing!

THE U.S. CUSTOM HOUSE

It was the Dutch who first settled on Manhattan, which they called New Amsterdam. One of the first buildings to be erected was a fort. You can still see a plaque on the U.S. Custom House at 1 Bowling Green (at the foot of Broadway) which gives some of the details about Fort New Amsterdam. But the plaque doesn't tell the whole story. The Dutch landed in 1624; two years later they began building the fort. That same year, 1626, the first Negro slaves were brought to Manhattan from Africa. They built the fort and performed other labors in the settlement. When necessary, they joined with the militia to fight hostile Indians.

Work on the fort went slowly; it was not until 1635 that Fort New Amsterdam was completed. At that time, the water line came up as far as today's State Street, and the fort commanded a view of both the North (or Hudson) and East Rivers. The main gate opened on Bowling Green. In 1642, the Church of St. Nicholas was built inside the fort. It was here that a Negro saved the city from destruction in 1689. The fact is recorded in colonial documents which are still in existence and readily available today in most New York libraries.

In 1689 the English were in control of the settlement. They had seized it from the Dutch in 1664 and changed the name to New York. Jacob Leisler was the governor at that time. On August 20, he sent a letter to King William and Queen Mary of England that told how the city was saved. In part, this is what he wrote:

> I have immediately proceeded to the proclaiming [of a day for prayer and thanksgiving] which was solemnly effected the 22nd day of June [1689] when we had miraculous deliverance of a fire which had been kindled in three places upon the turret of the church in the fort; 6,000 pounds of powder being next under the same roof and suspected to be done by one Papist who had been there before and was discovered by one Negro. Fort, city and the people were, through God's mercy, saved from that devilish design.

Unfortunately, the name of that brave and quick-witted Negro was never recorded. Evidence that there was a church in Fort New Amsterdam came to light when the fort was demolished in 1690 to make room for a government house. Workers found the church cornerstone with this inscription on it:

Year of Our Lord 1642, N. Kief, Director General, hath caused the congregation to erect this temple.

The members of that first group of Negroes did not spend all their lives in servitude. On their petition, they were freed and given grants of land. Not all early Negroes in Manhattan were brought to the island as laborers. Some came and stayed of their own free will. Dutch records disclose that in 1647 a land grant was given to one Jan Negro "who came with the privateer." Since Negroes had sailed to the New World with Columbus and other explorers, it is not unlikely that there were many earlier "Jan Negroes."

BOWLING GREEN

Facing 1 Broadway is a small, round park. The iron fence around it was built in 1771, but the park was being used much earlier. Inside the park there is a statue of Abraham de Peyster, an early official of New York. In the late seventeenth century (1699, to be exact), the governor was Richard Coote, Lord Bellemont. He sent a letter to the Board of Trade in London that shows an interesting view of life in New York at that time. Bellemont

had been ordered by the King of England to convert the
Negroes and Indians to Christianity. His letter, written,
perhaps, while he sunned himself in the Bowling Green,
which was used as the governors' garden, explained why
he had not complied with the King's request. Part of that
letter follows:

> They [the white settlers] have a notion that Negroes
> being converted to Christianity would emancipate
> them from their services, for they [the settlers] have
> no other servants in this country but Negroes.

At that time, many people felt it was very wrong for
one Christian to enslave another.

CASTLE CLINTON

The low, round building in Battery Park is called
Castle Clinton. As the plaque on it explains, Castle Clinton was first a fort. In 1824 it was converted into a place
for meetings and entertainment. It was then called
Castle Garden. In 1852 it became an immigrant station.
From 1896 to 1941 it housed the Aquarium, which is now
located in Coney Island. Although known today as
Castle Clinton, as Castle Garden it has a place in the
history of the Negro in New York.

A public mass meeting was held in Castle Garden on
October 30, 1850. The meeting was arranged by a group
of white merchants called the Union Safety Committee.
Their object was to persuade the public to accept the

Castle Clinton in Battery Park as it looks today.

Compromise of 1850, which Congress had passed in an effort to settle the question of slavery in the United States. The merchants hoped to stop the agitation over slavery which had caused several slave states to threaten to secede from the Union. The New York merchants were afraid that secession would have a bad effect on their business.

Merchants who refused to go along with the mass meeting suffered a loss in business. One firm took a stand which set an example that shines brightly to this very day. Bowen & McNamee, a silk goods firm at 16 William Street, took out ads proclaiming, "Our goods and not our principles are on the market."

Another historic event took place at Castle Garden in 1851. An official city reception was held for the Hungarian revolutionary leader, Louis Kossuth. He had been brought to the United States as a guest on the battleship *Mississippi*. Several days later, a delegation of Negroes was received by Kossuth. The delegation included John Zuille, Phillip Bell, Dr. J. M. Smith and George T. Downing, who acted as spokesman. Downing conveyed to Kossuth the sympathy of the Negro people in New York and their hopes that the Hungarian peasants would win their freedom. He also pointed out that the victory would be welcomed by all mankind. Kossuth listened politely, but there was little he could say or do since he was a guest of the United States, where the Constitution itself sanctioned slavery.

LOWER NEW YORK BAY

Walk from Castle Clinton to the railing at the water. This gives an unhampered view of the shoreline across the bay. It was easy for the soldiers in the Revolutionary War to join forces when the Battle of Long Island took place in 1776. Oliver Cromwell of the Second New Jersey Regiment of the Continental Army was one of the thousands of Negroes who helped win independence for the United States. He served for six years and received his discharge personally from General George Washington. After the war, he lived in Burlington, New Jersey. The Burlington *Gazette* had an interview with Cromwell on his hundredth birthday.

Philip Fields, who died in service, was among the Negro New Yorkers at Valley Forge with Washington and crossed the Delaware River with him. Details of some of the Negroes' war experiences can be found in their applications for pensions.

STATEN ISLAND

Although it is much closer to New Jersey, Staten Island is part of New York City. It can be seen from Battery Park. Until recently, the only way to get there was by ferry, but now there's a magnificent new bridge, the Verrazano Narrows Bridge, connecting Staten Island and Brooklyn.

During the Revolutionary War, a Negro named Bill Richmond lived on Staten Island (also called the Borough of Richmond or Richmond County, after the British duke of Richmond). While the British were in control of New York, three Hessian soldiers attacked Richmond and were soundly beaten by him. That affair brought Richmond to the attention of the Duke of Northumberland. Boxing was a popular sport in London and the Duke was an ardent sportsman. When the war was over, he took Richmond to London, where the Negro became a leading figure in the world of sports. Richmond opened a tavern in London and remained there. In his later years he coached and trained Tom Molineaux, a Negro who became the first unofficial heavyweight boxing champion of the United States.

THE STATUE OF LIBERTY

Probably the most famous landmark in the whole world is the queen of New York Harbor, the Statue of Liberty. It was a gift from the people of France to the people of the United States. The statue is connected with two significant events in the history of American Negroes.

The Statue of Liberty was not the first gift from the French to the Americans. In 1860 a collection was taken up by the French people after the execution of John Brown, a white man who seized a Government arsenal at Harper's Ferry in 1859. He and his two sons and other followers hoped to free the slaves. But they were cap-

A reproduction of an old picture postcard showing the Statue of Liberty and signed by the sculptor, Bartholdi.

SOUVENIR D'UNE VISITE AUX TRAVAUX DE LA STATUE DE LA LIBERTÉ
EXÉCUTÉE PAR A. BARTHOLDI

tured, tried and convicted of treason. After the execution, the famous French author, Victor Hugo, started a collection which paid for a gold medal which was presented to John Brown's widow. Again, when Abraham Lincoln was assassinated, the French people collected money for a gold medal that was presented to Mrs. Lincoln. The medal was inscribed, and part of the inscription read, "He saved the Union without veiling the statue of liberty." One of the people who observed the enthusiasm of the French in raising money for gifts was a sculptor named Bartholdi. The phrase "statue of liberty" inspired him to create one. He became a leader in the plan to present such a statue to the United States. Eventually, he was the one chosen to design it.

These two events, John Brown's Raid and Lincoln's assassination, both of which are so important to Negro history, paved the way for the collection of money for the Statue of Liberty.

FRAUNCES TAVERN

The oldest landmark of Revolutionary days still standing in New York City is Fraunces Tavern at Pearl and Broad Streets. Its owner was Samuel Francis, a French West Indian Negro. He changed his name to Fraunces and opened a tavern that was to become world famous. In the early days, the Liberty Boys plotted the Revolution there, the New York Chamber of Commerce was organized there, and General Washington said farewell to his officers in the Long Room of the Tavern. "Black

*The original Fraunces Tavern, in the early days
before it was enlarged and restored.*

Sam's" daughter, Phoebe, saved the life of the General. She stopped him from eating food poisoned by one of his bodyguards, Thomas Hickey, who was later hanged. Sam Fraunces was appointed steward of the first Presidential mansion after Washington was elected. The nation's capital was in New York at that time. When it was moved to Philadelphia, Fraunces continued his duties in the new capital. He died there in 1795, leaving a will that revealed that the Federal Government and several states owed him money for feeding and housing troops during the Revolution.

Fraunces Tavern now contains a public museum and has a dining room open to the public. The building is owned by the Sons of the Revolution, and is used as their meeting place.

HANOVER SQUARE

Just around the corner from the Tavern is Hanover Square and William Street. A plaque on the wall of the Cotton Exchange there marks the spot where William Bradford was appointed public printer in 1693. Bradford printed a newspaper called the *Gazette*. One early issue called for a collection to ransom white sailors held in slavery on the Barbary Coast of Africa. Another issue offered Negroes, Welshmen, cheese and other commodities for sale. Ads which offered rewards for the capture of Negro and white fugitives from labor were common in newspapers until the Civil War.

DOWNING'S OYSTER HOUSE

No tour of New York would be complete without mention of Downing's Oyster House, at 3-7 Broad Street at the corner of Wall Street. The site is now occupied by the Morgan Guaranty Trust Company building. For forty-six years, from 1820 to 1866, Thomas Downing owned and operated his famous restaurant. He was a native of Virginia who came to New York City shortly after the War of 1812. His specialty was pickled oysters, and he received a gold watch from Queen Victoria in return for sending her a barrel of his oysters. It was here that his son, George T. Downing, learned the restaurant business.

Cider and vinegar from his huge cellars were used to help put out the great fire in New York in 1835. Downing's quick thinking in this major catastrophe was recognized by many authorities, including A. E. Costello in his book, *Our Firemen.* Costello said that Downing's action saved a great deal of the surrounding property from total destruction.

His cellar was also a station on the Underground Railway. When Charles Dickens made a tour of New York in 1842, a former mayor, Philip Hone, asked Downing to supervise all the food and service at a gala reception held in the author's honor.

Descendants of Thomas Downing still live in the city, and they have many old newspaper clippings about their famous ancestor.

THE NEW YORK STOCK EXCHANGE

The New York Stock Exchange was formed by commission brokers who once met under a buttonwood tree which stood on the site of what is now 60 Wall Street. Even though Negroes had little control over their own destinies during the slavery period in the United States, they still sometimes managed to affect the course of history.

In 1709, official decree set up a slave market in New York City. The market was near the buttonwood tree at 60 Wall Street. The tree was also close to the Tontine Coffee House at Wall and Water Streets. It was there that the "Peep-o-Day Boys" would wait to see ships come into the Harbor. New York Harbor was a chief port for slave ships at that time. Before the Thirteenth Amendment of 1865, slavery was entirely within the Constitution, and the slave trade was regarded by many as a perfectly respectable business. The fortunes of several of today's noted families had their foundation in the slave trade.

Alexander Hamilton was the man who got the brokers from under the buttonwood tree. He was the first Secretary of the Treasury. Hamilton proposed that the Federal Government assume the debts of the states that had piled up during the Revolutionary War. Since the Federal Government had no money to pay off these debts, Hamilton suggested that bonds be issued which would be sold to the public. The commission brokers signed an agreement among themselves which set up the Stock

Exchange. They also agreed on the commission rate they would charge to act as middlemen in the disposal of the Government bonds to the public. In order to get the approval of Congress, it was necessary to compromise with representatives of the slave states. They wanted the nation's capital out of New York and closer to the geographical center of the country. The deal was made—the capital was moved to Philadelphia. Eventually, Virginia and Maryland each gave a piece of land for a national capital, and the District of Columbia came into being.

THE FIRST INSURANCE COMPANIES

A plaque on the wall of the building located at 58 Wall Street identifies it as the site of the first insurance companies in the United States. One of the early companies at that address was the Nautilus Company. The death of Philip Swan in 1846 represented the company's first loss on a policy. Swan was a Negro slave owned by Fred Clarke of Powhatan, Virginia. Clarke, who had taken out the policy, was the beneficiary. The Nautilus Company is now known as the New York Life Insurance Company.

TRINITY CHURCH

On Broadway at Wall Street, in the heart of New York's financial district, stands Trinity Church, the oldest Episcopal house of worship in the city. It received a royal charter from the King of England in 1697, becom-

The original Trinity Church, before it was enlarged twice.

ing the Church of England in the New York Colony. At that time, no other religion was permitted, and there was great prejudice against Catholics, Jews and Quakers. Trinity received vast amounts of land in the city. By 1776, its graveyard held thousands of bodies. The church became immensely wealthy. Negroes worshiped there in an area set apart from the main congregation.

In 1857 a Select Committee of the Legislative Assembly of New York was appointed to investigate the corporate affairs of Trinity. The committee learned that the church was not living up to its original charter, which stated that Trinity was supposed to encourage smaller parishes so the Church of England could spread its influence throughout the area. The church held mortgages valued at $600,000 on small parish churches, some of which had to close because of lack of money. The committee also learned that Trinity had declined to assist a Negro parish which had asked for $100. The legislature tried to encourage Trinity to share its wealth with less fortunate churches. Old records at Trinity reveal that its rectors performed many marriages between Negro couples.

THE JOHN STREET METHODIST CHURCH

At 44 John Street, between Nassau and William Streets, is the John Street Methodist Church. Formed in 1766 on Horse and Cart Lane (now William Street) it is

the oldest Methodist church in the United States. A picture of its first sexton, Peter Williams, hangs on a wall
in the church basement. Williams was a slave whose
owner left this country rather than support the Revolution. The church purchased Williams and let him buy
his own freedom. He was a tobacconist and an undertaker. Williams earned a good living in his shop at 239
Orange Street. He was so highly regarded by Methodist
historians that one church history—Wakeley's—devotes
three chapters to him. His wife, Molly, earned a small
measure of fame because she enjoyed helping to pull the
fire engine of Hanover Square Company 11.

In 1796, Peter Williams and other Negro members of
the John Street Church formed the first Negro-led church
in New York City. It was called Mother African Methodist Episcopal Zion Church, sometimes referred to as
Mother A.M.E. Zion or just Mother Zion Church. It is
still in existence today and is now located in Harlem. In
the early nineteenth century, it furnished the meeting
place and the inspired leadership for Negro New Yorkers.

Negro members of the First Baptist Church on Gold
Street also became disenchanted with the segregated
practices of the early churches in the city. They founded
the Abyssinian Baptist Church in 1808. Out of the early
Abyssinian Church grew Concord Baptist Church in
Brooklyn. Both of these churches are still very much in
existence, and they claim the largest Protestant congregations of any churches in the United States.

MARY WASHINGTON

A large building at 79 John Street, between Gold and Nassau Streets, now occupies the site that was once the home of a well-known and highly respected Negro, Mary Washington. While she was also known as Chloe and Mary Simpson, contemporary city directories referred to her as Mary Washington, fruiterer. She sold fruit and vegetables from a little shop in the basement of the building for thirty years. A local newspaper, the *Metropolitan*, carried her obituary when she died on March 27, 1836.

Mary Washington was a slave in the New York household of George Washington. He freed her and also gave her some personal mementos, including a small trunk with his initials on it. While Washington was still alive, she began annual celebrations of his birthday because she was afraid he might soon be forgotten. On that day, she would place her Washington souvenirs on a large table, and people of all sorts would drop in to share the occasion. William Dunlap, a famous artist of the time, painted a miniature of Mary Washington, but unfortunately it has been lost. On her death, she bequeathed her estate to St. George's Episcopal Church, which was then at Beekman and Cliff Streets.

LEWIS H. LATIMER

A plaque on 257 Pearl Street explains that Thomas Edison built the first powerhouse in America on the

A modern artist's conception of Mary Washington. An earlier painting of her by William Dunlap has disappeared.

site. This powerhouse produced electrictiy for lighting streets and homes. The first textbook on the Edison lighting system was written in 1890 by a Negro, Lewis H. Latimer. By hard work and study, Latimer, the son of a fugitive slave, became a draftsman, inventor, artist, poet and author. Latimer was a charter member of the Edison Pioneers, a group of men described as the creators of the electric industry. The telephone industry also owes thanks to Latimer—he wrote the description and drew the plans of the telephone so that Alexander Graham Bell could receive a patent for his invention. A Brooklyn public school is named after Latimer.

GRANVILLE T. WOODS

Thomas Edison had high regard for another Negro inventor, Granville T. Woods. During Edison's lifetime, an Ohio newspaper described Woods as "the equal, if not the superior, of any living inventor." Woods was sued by Edison on several occasions and, each time, Woods established in the U.S. Patent Court his right to patents on inventions that Edison claimed as his own. Edison offered Woods an extremely well-paying position in his laboratory, but Woods preferred to market his own inventions. He invented the "third rail," the electric distributor, the electric safety cutout, a method for sending telegraph messages between moving trains, and a system for sending as many as two hundred telegraph messages over a single wire in opposite directions. Woods invented other devices that made railroad travel safer, and they were used on the Manhattan Elevated Railway as well

Granville T. Woods (1856–1910), famous inventor.

as on railroads throughout the country. At the turn of the twentieth century, every Bell telephone used his transmitter.

Woods was a New York resident at the time of his death in 1910. He is buried in St. Michael's Cemetery in Astoria, Queens. It is interesting to note that Woods dropped out of school when he was ten, but he had the good judgment to go back when he was twenty.

JAMES HAMLET

Now at 58 Water Street, between Cuyler's Alley and Old Slip, is an old Grace Midland Trust Company building. But in 1850, the premises were occupied by the firm of Tilton & Maloney. The porter for the firm was a well-respected Negro, James Hamlet. He was the first known Negro in New York to be seized under the Fugitive Slave Act of 1850. On September 30 of that year, a Baltimore slave-catcher named Clare seized Hamlet from his job.

According to Clare's testimony before the Federal Commissioner, Hamlet was the fugitive slave of Mary Brown of Baltimore and she wanted him back. Hamlet was ordered back, and the Commissioner received a Federal fee of $10. Had he not been returned, the Commissioner's fee would have been $5. Hamlet was on his way to Baltimore before his family and friends learned anything about the case. Under the law, Hamlet could not even testify in his own defense.

On October 1, 1850, a mass meeting for James Hamlet was held in Mother Zion Church. Many sympathetic white people attended. George T. Downing offered resolutions which were presented to city officials. A collection was taken up to ransom Hamlet, a common practice in those days. White members of the Union Safety Committee contributed to the fund, and a Negro named Isaac Hollenbeck donated $100 to the cause. It was a white businessman, John H. Woodgate, who went to Baltimore and ransomed Hamlet for $800. Hamlet returned to New York, his family and his job.

The kidnapping of Negroes by slave-catchers became so frequent that New York City Negroes formed a Vigilante Committee of Thirteen. Their objectives were to prevent kidnappings and to give assistance to fugitive slaves. White citizens of good will gave their support to the work of the Committee of Thirteen. George T. Downing was one of the members, and his brother-in-law, Dr. John de Grasse, was another. The doctor's brother was Isaiah de Grasse, an early Episcopal minister. Both were sons of Count Georges de Grasse, the Hindu foster son of Admiral Count de Grasse, whose fleet turned the tide to American victory at Yorktown during the Revolutionary War.

COENTIES SLIP

Coenties Slip is one short block from the place where James Hamlet was kidnapped. On the wharf at Coenties Slip, Negro slaves of New York competed for entertainment honors against other Negroes from Long Island and New Jersey. On Saturday evenings, crowds would gather to watch talented performers. They sang, danced and drew hauntingly beautiful music from unusual instruments. The coins tossed their way by the spectators undoubtedly made life less harsh for those people in bondage.

MAIDEN LANE

On Maiden Lane, near a pond at William Street, the first organized revolt of Negro slaves in New York took place in 1712. Contrary to popular belief, at no time did Negroes meekly submit to being enslaved. As individuals and as groups, they acted with reckless courage to regain their freedom. Since they came from about six hundred different African tribes and spoke almost as many different dialects, it was difficult for them even to communicate with each other. Nonetheless, on April 12, 1712, about thirty slaves made a desperate bid for freedom. They inflicted much damage on persons and property before the militia chased them into the woods behind Maiden Lane. There, several committed suicide. The rest were soon captured and brutally executed as an example to other slaves. Harsh laws were drawn up in efforts to prevent more uprisings, but they could not quell the desire for freedom.

PART TWO

CITY HALL

JUST north of the Battery Park area is City Hall. Not only are city office buildings in this area, but there are state and Federal office buildings, too. The streets, like those further south, are narrow and seem to have been laid out without any sort of plan. This is quite true; no one planned how the streets should run in lower Manhattan. That explains why it is so easy to get lost in that area. But getting "lost" on a walking tour is a good way to stumble upon new streets and discover interesting bits of history.

EARLY NEGRO BURIAL GROUND

Two hundred years ago, the section at Chambers Street and Broadway was well outside the limits of New York City. Part of City Hall Park was a burial ground for Negroes. Catholics and Jews were also buried outside the city until the prejudice against them abated. Close by what is now City Hall, executions were carried out by both the Dutch and the English.

Engraving of City Hall in 1826 by I. J. Hill.

In Dutch colonial times there was a hangman named "Black Peter." Once, when he was performing his duty on a Negro called Big Manuel, the rope broke. As Black Peter attempted to try again, the large crowd that had come to witness the execution cried out in protest, and Big Manuel was set free. He lived to become part owner of what is now Greenwich Village. There were other services that Black Peter rendered to the city. In 1662, he submitted a bill to the city for a whipping he inflicted upon two Dutchmen for stealing cabbages. When no public hangman was available, the Dutch had a custom of giving freedom to a slave who carried out an execution.

The northeast corner of Broadway and Chambers Street was the location of New York's first large department store, the A. T. Stewart Bazaar. During the excavation for the building in the middle of the nineteenth century, many human skeletons were found. Some people thought they were the remains of Revolutionary War veterans, but it is more probable that they were among the hundreds of cholera victims of the epidemic of 1770. Before proper sewer and water systems were installed, cholera and other diseases took the lives of thousands of New Yorkers. At such times, wealthy people fled to the country north of what is now Canal Street.

It is ironic that Jacob Leisler, the Governor of New York when the unknown Negro saved the city from destruction in 1689, was hanged for treason at Broadway and Chambers Street. He was buried in a corner of his garden which was just about where Nassau Street ends today.

THE ALMSHOUSE

Public buildings, such as jails and the Almshouse, were all close to what is now City Hall. In 1827, a Negro newspaper, *Freedom's Journal*, had a census of the people in the Almshouse. It revealed that 1,351 white men, women and children were in the poorhouse as compared with eighty-one Negro men, women and children.

The same issue of the *Journal* carried the "Memoirs of Paul Cuffee," a Massachusetts Negro who was a merchant, shipowner and shipbuilder. While protesting taxation without representation, and the lack of schools for Negro children, he built a school and hired teachers. In 1815, he took thirty-eight Negro families to Africa in his own ship and at his own expense.

CITY HALL

The day-to-day business of the city is conducted at City Hall. The public may see the Mayor and the Board of Estimate in action. The present Secretary of the Board of Estimate is Mrs. Ruth Whitehead Whaley, a Negro lawyer who has held this post for many years.

PRINTING HOUSE SQUARE

To the east of City Hall, facing the park, is Printing House Square. At the point where Nassau and Spruce Streets join with Park Row, there is a statue of Benjamin

Franklin. This area of the city once abounded with printers and publishers. In 1787, Franklin became the first president of the first Anti-Slavery Society in the United States. Two years later he presented a petition to Congress for the abolition of the slave trade. On March 12, 1790, using the pseudonym "Historicus," Franklin wrote a satirical article in the *Federal Gazette* in which, using the arguments of slave owners, Franklin justified the enslavement of white people.

CURRIER AND IVES

The building at 115 Nassau Street, at the corner of Spruce Street, was occupied by Currier and Ives. Their lithographs were extremely popular in the mid-nineteenth century, and they are collectors' items today. Their pictures showed life in the United States and famous people of their time. While they usually portrayed Negroes in a comic vein, the only picture we have of the first group of Negro United States Representatives and Senators was their work.

THE HARMON FOUNDATION

The offices and art gallery of the Harmon Foundation were at 140 Nassau Street for many decades. After years of helping Negro artists to achieve recognition, the organization has closed its doors because its major aim has been achieved. This aim, to have Negro artists receive the recognition they deserve, has been achieved mostly through the efforts of its director, Mary Brady. She is probably one of the world's greatest authorities on Negro artists of the United States and Africa.

VAUX HALL GARDENS

In the late eighteenth century, the area from Chambers to Warren Streets and west toward the North (Hudson) River, was covered by Vaux Hall Gardens. This was a tea garden owned by Sam Fraunces of Fraunces Tavern. Wax statues dotted the spacious lawn facing the river, where in the summer New Yorkers sipped their drinks and nibbled on delicate pastries. After Fraunces abandoned Vaux Hall Gardens, several other places in the city adopted that name.

KATY FERGUSON

The home of a beloved Negro, Catherine (Katy) Ferguson, was at 51 Warren Street. She is listed in early city directories as a pastrymaker. In 1853 she owned a pastry shop at 74 Thompson Street, just off Canal Street. She died in 1854 shortly before the city Almshouse burned down. During her active lifetime, Mrs. Ferguson "adopted" twenty white children and twenty-eight Negro children from the Almshouse. She raised them until she could find homes or jobs for them. One of her foster children was Isaac Ferris, a chancellor of the nineteenth-century New York City University, now New York University. Ferris held that position from 1852 to 1870.

Both Cubberly's *History of Education* and Benson Lossing's *Lives of Eminent Americans* give credit to Mrs. Ferguson for founding the Sunday School movement in New York City. The Katy Ferguson Home, formerly in Harlem but now on Staten Island, is a continuing memorial to her fine work. Mrs. Ferguson's own mother was sold as a slave when Katy was only eight years old.

DAVID RUGGLES

In 1838, a Negro sailor named David Ruggles lived at 36 Lispenard Street. The famous abolitionist, Samuel May, credited Ruggles with helping at least six hundred slaves to escape to freedom on the Underground Railroad. Ruggles traveled both by land and by sea whereever his services could relieve the suffering of enslaved people. He was forced to give up his work when he lost his sight. He received support from friends, but he did not like being dependent upon anyone. He leased a house in Northampton, Massachusetts with the help of friends in the anti-slavery movement. Ruggles converted the house into a water-cure hospital, which helped him to support himself and his family the rest of his life.

Some other Negro sailors also worked as "conductors" on the Underground Railroad. Going to sea was one occupation open to educated Negroes during the slavery period in the United States. Consequently, there were Negro seamen who could outwit the slave owners. Sometimes, however, their efforts were not completely successful. In 1859, three Negro sailors, Johnson, Garsey and Eason, helped a slave named Isaac to escape from Norfolk, Virginia. They got him safely to New York, but slave-catchers from Virginia caught him and returned Isaac to slavery. Governor Wise of Virginia offered a $3,000 reward to anyone who would bring the three seamen to Virginia for punishment. Although there were both Negroes and white men in New York who would and could do such things, the three sailors were never caught.

NATIONAL ASSOCIATION OF COLORED WOMEN

Organized in 1896, the National Association of Colored Women had its offices at 9 Murray Street. It was the pioneer national organization of Negro women. Some of the officers in 1897 were Mary Church Terrel of Washington, D.C., who was the first Negro member of the American Association of College Women; Frances Jackson Coppin, the educator who has had several schools named for her; and Mrs. Booker T. Washington of Alabama, the wife of the famous Negro educator and builder of Tuskegee Institute.

Further up Murray Street, at numbers 41-47, was the Third Associate Presbyterian Church. The Reverend Dr. John M. Mason, the pastor, was so impressed by the crowd of children that Katy Ferguson gathered in her home for Bible lessons on Sundays that he made room for her Sunday School in his church.

DUN AND BRADSTREET

The home of the famous credit rating firm, Dun and Bradstreet, is at 99 Church Street. The credit rating business in America was started by an abolitionist named Arthur Tappan, who had a silk goods firm at 122 Pearl Street. He lost his money when he was caught between merchants who disliked his abolitionist sentiments and the depression of 1837. He turned to using his customer lists to provide merchants with information about the credit standing of prospective customers. Business flourished and Tappan expanded the firm to take in his brother, Lewis, and other employees. Among the newcomers was an enterprising young man named Robert Graham Dun. Tappan retired a wealthy man and devoted his time, energy and wealth to anti-slavery activities. Dun continued the business, merging in later years with the Bradstreet Company. The Tappan brothers also founded the New York *Journal of Commerce*, the forerunner of the *Wall Street Journal*.

PIERRE TOUSSAINT

Just a few steps from Dun and Bradstreet, at Church and Barclay Streets, stands St. Peter's Catholic Church, the first in New York City after Catholics were permitted to worship in public. Almost from the very start, pew number 25 belonged to a pious Negro named Pierre Toussaint. There is a large bronze tablet in front of the church dedicated to his memory.

Toussaint was a hairdresser on Chapel Street (now West Broadway). In his later life, he bought a house on Franklin Street, which he used as an orphanage. People from all over the city would write to him asking for help. The main branch of the New York Public Library (Fifth Avenue at 42nd Street) has many of these letters. It may be said that Toussaint was the city's first social worker. Several books have been written about him, and a motion picture biography of Pierre Toussaint is under consideration.

Paintings of Toussaint, his wife and his niece can be seen at the New-York Historical Society (170 Central Park West). When he died in 1853, all New York mourned him.

FREEDOM'S JOURNAL

The first newspaper in the United States owned and published by Negroes was *Freedom's Journal,* with offices at 150 Church Street. The owners were John Russworm and the Reverend Samuel Cornish, both highly educated men. Russworm was probably the first Negro to graduate from an American college. He received a bachelor's degree from Bowdoin College in 1826. Three years later he earned a master's degree at the same college.

It was a great disappointment to Negroes when Russworm went to Liberia in 1829. He accepted an appointment from the American Colonization Society to become

the governor of Maryland Province in Africa. This later
became a part of Liberia. The vast majority of American
Negroes opposed schemes to colonize free Negroes outside their native land. They felt that they and their
ancestors had helped to build this country and that it was
wrong to suggest that they should leave. Besides, only
free Negroes were encouraged to migrate, which would
leave the majority still enslaved in the United States.

Russworm never returned to America. *Freedom's
Journal* stopped publication in 1829, but Cornish soon
had another newspaper going. Since then there have
been at least a dozen Negro newspapers published by
New Yorkers. They all served the same purpose as the
foreign-language newspapers that are published by and
for different ethnic groups in New York.

THE MUNICIPAL BUILDING

The gigantic New York City Municipal Building
straddles Chambers Street at Centre Street like a steel
and concrete colossus. Ferdinand Q. Morton, a lawyer,
was the first Negro to serve as a Civil Service Commissioner. Probably the longest tenure of any New York City
Commissioner was held by Arthur Ford, a Negro, who
was Commissioner of Water Supply, Gas and Electricity
from 1954 until 1966, when he retired. Commissioner
Ford was a civil engineer by profession.

In recent years, many Negroes have held highly re-
sponsible positions in New York City government.

Fire Commissioner Robert Lowery.

Among these distinguished officials are the present Fire
Commissioner, Robert Lowery, and the Borough Presi-
dent of Manhattan, Percy Sutton, as well as three earlier
Borough Presidents of Manhattan—Hulan Jack, Edward
Dudley and Constance Motley. Mr. Dudley is now a
judge of the New York State Supreme Court, and Mrs.
Motley is a Federal judge.

In 1917, Edward Johnson, a teacher and author of
books on Negro history, became the first Negro member of the Legislative Assembly of New York. He was
also an uncle of Judge Edward Dudley.

MOTHER AFRICAN METHODIST
EPISCOPAL ZION CHURCH

The first church built in New York City by and for
Negroes was Mother A.M.E. Zion Church at 156 Church
Street, at the corner of Leonard Street. Money for the
land and for much of the cost of the building was donated by Peter Williams, the tobacconist and undertaker
mentioned earlier. He laid the cornerstone on July 30,
1800. The congregation now worships in its own church
in Harlem.

In September, 1833, a disastrous fire ruined the original building. The fire had started in the National Theater
across Leonard Street, and the flames spread to several
buildings nearby. Some of the buildings were destroyed
along with the theater and the church, but Mother Zion

was the only one that was fully insured. Consequently, the congregation was able to rebuild the church on the same site within a short time.

In the nineteenth century, the neighborhood surrounding Mother Zion Church was a curious mixture of religious, cultural and residential buildings. Some of them had very poor reputations because of the activities that went on inside. Both Negroes and white people lived in the area, and they, too, were a mixture of good and bad. One of the more notorious Negroes was Pete Williams (no relation to Peter Williams of Mother Zion), who had a dance hall and saloon on Leonard Street. It was called the Dickens Place in honor of the celebrated English author, Charles Dickens, who visited the neighborhood in 1842. In the 1850's Mother Zion had a burial ground at what is now 85th Street between Seventh and Eighth Avenues.

At present, near the original site of Mother Zion, there is a cooperative housing development. One of the residents is Harold Williams, a direct descendant of Mother Zion's founder. From his terrace, Harold Williams can see where his ancestors lived and worshiped in the eighteenth and nineteenth centuries.

THE FIVE POINTS DISTRICT

The Five Points District was behind what is now the New York State Office Building at 80 Centre Street. The location is marked by a statue of Christopher Columbus at the point where Bayard and Worth Streets meet. In the early 1800's, Five Points was the center of New York's Negro population, complete with homes, schools, churches and businesses. Poverty and an influx of persons with bad reputations, both white and Negro, made Five Points a notorious district. Gangs of white toughs dominated the area. Among them were the Dead Rabbits, the Bowery Boys, the Plug Uglies and the O'Connell Guards. During the Civil War draft riots in 1863, these gangs inflicted great damage on the persons and property of Negroes.

The Dutch governors of New York had issued many land grants to Negroes in the area. However, as the population of the city was increased by migration from Europe, Five Points became an area of degradation. An abandoned brewery became a hovel in which hundreds of people lived. One alley contained a long shed called the "Den of the Forty Thieves." People of all races and nationalities lived in it, and decent citizens went near it only at great risk.

One of the important factors that contributed to the notoriety of Five Points was the "Jackson Whites" and the "Jackson Blacks." According to one story, Jackson was a British agent during the Revolutionary War. He "imported" many women, white and Negro, from English prisons and West Indian slave plantations to the Five Points area. They were to be companions for the Hessian soldiers stationed there. After the war, the women were left behind, and they attracted the most unsavory characters in Manhattan to the area.

It would be wrong to condemn the entire population of Five Points because of the over-all reputation of the area. One of its outstanding citizens was David Broderick, a white stonecutter, who went to California during the Gold Rush of 1849. He was elected to the first Territorial Legislature, California's governing body before it became a state. In the struggle to decide whether California would enter the Union as a slave or free state, Broderick's voice was loud and clear in favor of freedom for all men. California was admitted to the Union as a free state in 1850. Six years later, Broderick was elected to the U.S. Senate from California. He was challenged to a duel in 1859 by a Southerner. He accepted even though he didn't know anything about dueling pistols. Broderick was fatally wounded, and his dying words, "They have killed me for opposing the extension of slavery," were used on banners during Lincoln's campaign for the Presidency in 1860.

The largest body of fresh water on Manhattan island, Fresh Water Pond (also known as Collect Pond), at one time covered part of the Five Points area. Eventually, the pond was drained and filled to make room for New York's growing population.

ST. PHILIP'S CHURCH

St. Philip's Church, now in Harlem, was founded by early Negro members of Trinity Church and its affiliate, St. Paul's Chapel. St. Philip's Episcopal Church was first built at 24 Collect Street. The street is now called Centre

Street, and the original site of the church is presently occupied by the U.S. Courthouse. St. Philip's, the first Negro Episcopal church, had a graveyard on Chrystie Street that was moved in 1885 to Cypress Hills Cemetery in Queens.

CHINATOWN

The area around Pell and Mott Streets was once known as "Little Africa." In 1858, Ah Ken was the first Chinese to move into Mott Street. Wa Kee soon moved into Pell Street, and before long a Chinese group called the On Leong Tong controlled Mott Street, and the Hip Sing Tong ruled Pell Street. Both tongs preyed on the hardworking Chinese residents of the area. Today, the Chinese, as a group, are perhaps the most law-abiding citizens of New York City.

THE AFRICAN RELIEF SOCIETY

Where the Traffic Court now stands, at 42 Baxter Street, was once the site of the first clubhouse of the New York African Society for Mutual Relief. The society was formed in 1786 despite the harsh penalties imposed at that time on Negroes caught meeting together. As the anti-slavery movement grew among white New Yorkers, the society began to meet more frequently to consider a more formal organization. The first real meeting took place in 1808 at the African Free School on Rose Street.

On this Baxter Street site, in 1810, the New York African Society built their clubhouse and Underground Railroad station.

William Hamilton, editor and publisher of the *Anglo-African* and other Negro newspapers, was elected president of the society.

The organizers of the society were highly respected men. All of them were industrious and some were wealthy. For example, Henry Scott of Scott & Company, of 217 Water Street, was one of the largest pickle manufacturers and wholesalers in the city. Thomas Downing owned and operated the Oyster House on Broad Street. Thomas Baggot was a grocer and soap manufacturer. Others were in the catering business. One, Thomas Jennings, invented a process for renovating clothes, and he had his own clothing store. Printers and bootmakers were also active members.

The primary objective of the society was to give the members and their families the financial security against sickness and death that many insurance companies denied them because of their race. In addition, they gave moral support and intellectual stimulation to one another. The members were also deeply concerned with the plight of the American Negro. Four of the society's members played a prominent part in the first National Convention of Colored People of the United States. It was held in Philadelphia in 1831. A member of the New York African Society, Henry Sipkins, was the president of that convention. The delegates considered ways and means to combat discrimination and the lack of equal opportunities for Negroes. They called upon the Federal Government to recognize that the Negro had a right to first-class citizenship equal to the responsibilities he was called upon to face.

The society was incorporated in 1810. Nine years later it bought the lot on Baxter Street and erected a building. Some time later it was sold at a good profit. When the building was demolished, a trap door was discovered leading to a secret room that was used as a station on the Underground Railroad. With the money from the sale of the Baxter Street property, the African Society purchased 27 Greenwich Avenue, which it rented out as a source of revenue.

Some years ago the society sold its last property at 43 West 66th Street. Members continue to keep the New York African Society active, and to maintain the charter, although the majority of the present members are octogenarians. On April 21, 1968, the society celebrated its 160th anniversary. It is probably the oldest mutual aid society in the country.

THE AFRICAN FREE SCHOOLS

The African Free School for Boys once stood at 137 Mulberry Street, in the heart of "Little Italy." The The African Free Schools were started by John Jay, Alexander Hamilton and other early abolitionists who were members of the Manumission Society. *The History of the African Free Schools in New York* by Charles Andrews, an early teacher, names many famous and prosperous graduates of these schools, including Ira Aldridge, the Shakespearean actor; George T. Downing, the restaurant owner; Alexander Crummell, the scholar and theologian, and many, many others.

Most of the pupils at these schools came from poor families. Early in the nineteenth century a group of Negro women formed an organization known as the African Dorcas Society. They scurried between the boys' school on Mulberry Street and the girls' school at 245 William Street. When they discovered children who were absent from school because they had no clothes to wear, the ladies provided clothing and saw to it that the children attended classes. Largely because of the efforts of the African Dorcas Society, a much higher proportion of Negro children attended school in New York City than did white children during that period.

St. Philip's Church and the New York Society for the Promotion of Education Among Colored Children supplemented the efforts of the African Free Schools. The Society was formed because the official group charged with the responsibility for public schools neglected those attended by Negro children. St. Philip's made available the basement of the church on Centre Street for a school, while the society organized another on Thomas Street. The latter school became Public School Number 6, and it followed the Negro population until segregated public schools were abolished in New York City in 1884.

OLD ST. PATRICK'S GRAVEYARD

The old St. Patrick's Cathedral Graveyard is at 263 Mulberry Street. It is here that Pierre Toussaint and his wife are buried. Their graves have been marked by an interracial Catholic society named for John Boyle O'Reilly, a Boston poet and friend of George Downing.

Toussaint's grave was located in 1953 by a priest, Father Charles McGahey. He was teaching in a small town in New Jersey and one of his pupils, a little Negro boy, refused to study. To combat this the priest went to a library to find someone the student could identify with and respect. By accident, Father McGahey learned of Toussaint and the fact that his burial place was unknown. Father McGahey undertook the task of locating the grave. When he succeeded, the late Cardinal Spellman of New York helped to have it suitably marked.

PART THREE

GREENWICH VILLAGE

NEW YORK'S Greenwich Village has long had a reputation for being the part of the city where the "young in heart" congregate. For generations it has been the traditional home of poets, musicians, writers and artists. Edgar Allan Poe and O. Henry lived there, and so have many other creative people.

In the very early days of the city, Greenwich Village was on its northern outskirts. The Dutch ceded land in the area to Negroes. During the nineteenth century, several of the Negroes who lived in the Village became quite well known in various fields. Among these were Charles L. Reason, the educator; George Downing, the restaurateur; Theodore Duplessis, noted far and near for his superlative ice cream; Mrs. Jeremiah Bowers, a leading dressmaker; and George Lawrence, one of the secretaries of the Haitian Legation.

As early as 1643, a free Negro, Domingo Anthony, lived in Greenwich Village, at that time hardly more than a swamp. In 1664 he was joined by several other Negroes who were released from servitude as a reward for years of faithful service. In December of the same year, Paul d'Angola, another Negro, received a grant to farm in Greenwich Village in order to pay off the price of his release. His farm included the land between Minetta Lane and Thompson Street. The path alongside Minetta Brook was called the Negro Causeway.

Big Manuel, who narrowly escaped being hanged some years before, received a grant covering much of what is now Washington Square Park. There were drawbacks to these land grants, however. They could be sold to pay off any debts left by a slave's former owner.

REVEREND J.W.C. PENNINGTON

The First Presbyterian Church was at the corner of Prince and Marion Streets. Its pastor was the Reverend J.W.C. Pennington, a fugitive slave who became a scholar. He traveled extensively in Europe and received his doctor of divinity degree from Heidelberg University in Germany. He was the author of an early history of the Negro in America.

The Reverend Pennington's church was in an area known in Dutch colonial times as the "free Negroes' lots." These stretched from Prince Street to Astor Place and from the Bowery to Broadway. Among the Negro landowners were Manuel Spangie and members of the Santomee family. Lucas Santomee was especially admired in his time for his skill as a physician.

Reverend Pennington was pastor of the First Presbyterian Church in 1826 when he performed the marriage ceremony of another fugitive slave—Frederick Douglass.

GEORGE T. DOWNING

The Oyster House owned and operated by George T. Downing was at 690 Broadway. His father, Thomas Downing, operated a restaurant at Broad and Wall Streets. From New York, the younger Downing branched out to Newport, Rhode Island, and he also operated a restaurant in the House of Representatives from 1865 to 1877.

When organized labor began to close its doors to Negroes, a National Negro Labor Union was formed. Although he was a wealthy man and in business for himself, Downing willingly accepted the vice-presidency of the Negro union. In 1859, he was chairman of the National Convention of Colored Men, which met in Boston. In one of his speeches to the group, he said, in part:

> The great consideration that presses upon me is what we may do to make ourselves of more importance in the community. . . . To sustain such a relation as this to the community (and it is possible) is to secure, beyond a question, all the respect and the enjoyment of all the rights that the most deferred to of this land enjoy. Society is deferential; it defers to POWER. Learning and wealth and power are most potent in society.

George Downing was born in New York City on December 30, 1819; he died in Newport, Rhode Island on July 21, 1903. During his lifetime he knew five Presidents of the United States and was well acquainted with

George Thomas Downing, of Rhode Island, famous restaurateur and labor leader.

almost all of the famous men of his day. He corresponded with some of them and kept their letters to him. The Downing Collection of autographed letters is now owned by a descendant of his living in New York City.

AFRICAN GROVE THEATER

The African Grove Theater was owned and operated by Negroes from about 1820 to 1830. The theater was at Mercer and Bleecker Streets. Each performance closed with a medley of operatic arias sung in a style that would do credit to any opera house. The African Grove Theater was finally forced to close by city authorities, who feared trouble from white toughs who had to sit in the gallery.

BUCKLEY'S ETHIOPIAN OPERA HOUSE

Buckley's Ethiopian Opera House, at 539 Broadway, was an extremely successful venture. Here white actors performed in blackface during the middle of the nineteenth century, and the audience loved it!

One of the great blackface actors of the early twentieth century was Eddie Leonard; few people knew that he was a Negro from Virginia. According to some accounts, his sister performed with Negro entertainment companies.

THE ISAAC T. HOPPER HOME

The Isaac T. Hopper Home, an organization that helps families in need, is located at 110 Second Avenue. It was founded in memory of Isaac T. Hopper, a white Quaker businessman and a staunch abolitionist. He personally helped to rescue at least one thousand Negroes from slavery in Philadelphia and in New York City. One of those he assisted was the Reverend Richard Allen, founder of the African Methodist Episcopal Church. Mr. Allen was a highly respected man in Philadelphia, but nonetheless he was arrested by a slave-catcher as a fugitive slave. There was a trial, but it didn't last long when it was proved that the fugitive slave had been missing for four years; Allen had been in Philadelphia for more than twenty years. The case against Allen was dismissed and upon the advice of Isaac Hopper, he sued the slave-catcher. The slave-catcher was sent to jail when he couldn't pay bail of $800. After three months, Allen had the charges dropped and the slave-catcher was released.

COOPER UNION INSTITUTE

The Great Hall of Cooper Union Institute is at Third Avenue and 7th Street. It was here that Abraham Lincoln made the speech that won him the Republican nomination for the Presidency in 1860. Frederick Douglass made the rafters ring on many occasions, and Wendell Phillips and other abolitionists also spoke here. The Cooper Union Institute was founded by Peter Cooper to

Commemorative medal honoring Isaac T. Hopper. The reverse is inscribed with the phrase, "To seek and to save that which was lost."

provide an education for impoverished young New
Yorkers who wanted to improve themselves.

ST. MARK'S IN-THE-BOWERY

The church that Peter Stuyvesant established, St.
Mark's in-the-Bowery, is at Second Avenue and 10th
Street. In his day, he worshiped here with about forty
Negro members of the church. Stuyvesant is buried in
the graveyard next to the church.

PART FOUR

UNION SQUARE AND MADISON SQUARE

ONE interesting thing about the squares of New York City is that they are more often round or rectangular than square in shape. Today Union Square runs from 14th to 16th Streets and from Fourth Avenue to Broadway. Now a highly commercial neighborhood with bustling shops of all kinds, it was the theatrical center of the city in by-gone days. As the legitimate theater moved further north, Union Square became an area notorious for its many burlesque houses.

It was at Union Square, on March 5, 1864, that the Union League Club of New York presented the colors to the first Negro New York Civil War volunteers. As early as 1861, the Negro citizens of New York pleaded for an opportunity to enlist in the New York regiments of the Union Army. Although the Confederacy used the services of Negroes, neither President Lincoln nor the northern states had called upon Negroes to enlist. Even after a shortage of personnel caused the ranks to open to Negroes in other states, New York failed to call for vol-

*1872 view of Union Square, looking east toward the
area now occupied by S. Klein's Department Store.
It was here that Negro regiments were massed to receive
regimental flags before going into the Civil War.*

unteers. As a result, Negroes went to other states to enlist.

Prominent white citizens organized a group called the New York Association for Colored Volunteers, which persuaded the governor of New York to allow Negroes to volunteer for the Union Army. They argued that Negroes were entitled to fight for freedom, that they were going to other states to enlist anyway, and that more white New Yorkers would have to be drafted if Negroes weren't allowed to fill the state's quota. The Negro regiment from New York had these words on its banners: "Rather Die a Free Man than Live to be a Slave."

During the First World War, the all-Negro 367th U.S. Regiment started from Union Square en route to Europe and to the war that was to "spread democracy over the world." Leo Pinckney of New York was a member of the 367th. When Americans were being selected for the draft, the first number was drawn in Washington, D.C. by Secretary of War Newton D. Baker. Pinckney, an obscure Negro, became famous overnight when his number was the first one picked. This made him the first American in history to be drafted to fight outside the United States.

THE FRIENDS' MEETING HOUSE

The Friends' Meeting House, at 15 Rutherford Place, is a Quaker house of worship. Although badly persecuted in early New York State, Quakers insisted on strict brotherhood, and they were always violently opposed to slavery.

ST. GEORGE'S EPISCOPAL CHURCH

St. George's Episcopal Church was once in the neighborhood where Mary Washington lived. This was the church to which Mary left her estate when she died. It is now at 207 East 16th Street, between Third Avenue and Stuyvesant Park.

The baritone soloist at St. George's for more than forty years was a Negro composer, Harry T. Burleigh. From 1900 until his death, he was also a member of the choir at Temple Emanu-El. Burleigh composed "Deep River," a classic in the concert field.

PRESIDENT THEODORE ROOSEVELT

Theodore Roosevelt was born at 28 East 20th Street. It was a coincidence that Roosevelt's term began just when the Congressional term of George White of North Carolina ended. He was the last of the southern Negroes elected to Congress during the Reconstruction period.

Roosevelt was a popular figure with his countrymen. He served in the Spanish-American War, in which five Negroes won the Congressional Medal of Honor and another Negro, Elijah B. Tunnel, was the first man to die.

President Roosevelt caused a sensation when he invited Booker T. Washington, the famous Negro educator, to dine at the White House. The President received a great deal of criticism for this, but Roosevelt said he would invite anyone he pleased to dine with him at the White House. However, in a letter to a friend, he described Booker T. Washington as "one of the occasionally good, well-educated, intelligent, honest colored men who should have the right to vote."

Although many of his words would indicate that Theodore Roosevelt had a strong belief in the existence of superior and inferior races, he also had a strong sense of fair play. When people in Indianola, Mississippi threatened the life of Mrs. Minnie Cox, the Negro postmistress of the town, President Roosevelt closed the post office immediately. And over the objections of the Senate, he appointed Dr. William Crum, a Negro, to be Collector of the Port of Charleston, South Carolina. It is likely, however, that the last act was done more out of stubbornness than fair play.

GRAMERCY PARK

Gramercy Park is located between Third Avenue and Park Avenue South (formerly Fourth Avenue), and extends from East 20th to East 21st Streets. It was only a swamp when Peter Stuyvesant's widow sold it to one of her former slaves.

MADISON SQUARE PARK

The almost rectangular area from Fifth Avenue and Broadway to Madison Avenue, and from 23rd to 26th Streets, is Madison Square Park. It is an area containing statues of people who were important to the history of the Negro.

In 1873, Roscoe Conkling was a Senator from New York when B. K. Bruce, a Negro, was elected to the U.S. Senate from Mississippi. According to custom, Bruce's Mississippi colleague should have escorted Bruce down the Senate aisle to take the oath of office. Bruce's fellow Senator from Mississippi refused to do so. As Bruce started his lonely walk, Roscoe Conkling leaped to his feet and escorted Bruce down the aisle. There is a public school in Brooklyn named for Senator Bruce, and a statue of Conkling is in Madison Square Park.

William Henry Seward was Abraham Lincoln's Secretary of State. Among his many important diplomatic achievements, Seward arranged the purchase of Alaska from Russia in 1867. When Harriet Tubman finished her work with the Underground Railroad, she retired to Auburn, New York. There, Seward sold her some land near his home. She built a home for aged colored women. Seward, too, is the subject of a Madison Square Park statue. Actually, it's Seward's head on Abraham Lincoln's body. Randolph Rogers, the sculptor, created a statue of Lincoln for a midwestern city that didn't pay for it. When the sculptor learned that New York City

Cover the head of this statue of Seward in Madison Square Park and the body of another great American—Abraham Lincoln—can easily be recognized.

was interested in a statue of Seward, he removed Lincoln's head and replaced it with Seward's.

Another statue honors David Farragut, the first full admiral in the United States Navy. He was also the hero of the Civil War Battle of Mobile Bay. It was on Farragut's recommendation that the Medal of Honor was awarded to John Lawson, a Negro sailor who served aboard the battleship *Hartford* during the Battle of Mobile Bay.

Chester Arthur, also the subject of a statue in Madison Square Park, practiced law before he became President of the United States. As a lawyer, he represented a Negro schoolteacher, Elizabeth Jennings, in court in a suit brought against the Third Avenue Railroad Company in 1854. The action was taken when Miss Jennings was forcibly removed from one of the railroad's horse-drawn cars simply because she was a Negro. Chester Arthur won the case against the railroad, and Miss Jennings received a settlement of $250. The significant point about this case is that after this, all New York City railroads, except one, ceased to discriminate against Negroes.

Madison Square Park is also the site of the Eternal Light, a monument dedicated to the Armed Forces of World War I. The first regiment to march past it was Harlem's 369th when it returned from Germany. Spectators were thrilled to see the first American soldiers to win the Croix de Guerre. The French Government had awarded this medal to Henry Johnson and Needham Roberts of the Harlem regiment.

MADISON SQUARE GARDEN

This world-famous sports and entertainment arena is now at Pennsylvania Station, its third location. Originally it was just outside Madison Square Park. In the spring of 1892, a Negro woman, Sissieretta Jones, held a concert there. Critics hailed her as the "Black Patti" because her voice and artistry equaled that of Adelina Patti, the most famous opera star of the day.

On April 5, 1917, another event took place there that is important to Negro history. Three one-act plays, written by a white man named Ridgely Torrence, were performed by a cast of Negroes. This was the first time Negroes performed serious dramas before the American public. The performance was a huge success. In 1898, Major Taylor made his debut at Madison Square Garden as a bicycle racer. He went on to become the world's champion cyclist.

THE NEW YORK COLORED MISSION

A privately supported institution, the New York Colored Mission was located at 135 West 30th Street in 1871. It contained a library, a reading room, lodgings and a trade school for Negroes who wanted to better themselves. In addition, it provided a free employment service and dispensed welfare to those in need.

SOLOMON PIETERS

The Flatiron Building, at 23rd Street where Broadway crosses Fifth Avenue, is on part of the thirty acres of land owned by a Negro, Solomon Pieters. He was one of the free Negroes who obtained land grants in Dutch colonial times. His will was probated in 1724 and is still part of the Manhattan Surrogate Court records. The will bequeathed to his wife and children "land, houses, silver-plate, tools of husbandry, money, etc."

PART FIVE

TIMES SQUARE

MOVIEGOERS the world over know that a picture of Times Square means the film they are about to see is set in New York City. The spectacular animated neon signs, the traffic and the thousands of people walking its streets daily seem to symbolize the action and brashness that is New York. It is not unusual for tens of thousands of people to jam into the area on New Year's Eve to welcome the new year with a roar that rattles window panes. The heart of the theater district and many first-run movie houses entice thousands of visitors from all over the world all year long. The native New Yorker may pretend to be unimpressed by the tinsel and glitter, but the area holds an enchantment for him, too.

RACIAL TROUBLE

The corner of 41st Street and Eighth Avenue was the scene of a race riot in 1900. The trouble started when a Negro shot a white man because the Negro suspected the stranger of molesting his wife. The wounded man was a popular policeman in plainclothes. For several days, mobs of white toughs roamed the streets looking for revenge against any Negro they met. Paul Laurence Dunbar, the famous Negro poet, was one of the injured. Negroes complained that they received no protection from the police during the disturbance.

It wasn't until 1911 that the consolidated police force of the five boroughs of New York City appointed its first Negro, Samuel Battle. He was a fine policeman who worked his way up through the ranks to become a lieutenant. When he retired from the force, he was appointed to the city's Parole Commission.

THE NEW YORK THEATER

In 1902, a company of Negroes produced a revue at the New York Theater on Broadway between 44th and 45th Streets. Titled "In Dahomey," the book was written by Jesse Shipp, the music was by Will Marion Cook and the lyrics by Paul Laurence Dunbar. The revue ran for a year, a very long time in those days. The stars were Bert Williams and George Walker. Williams was such a sensation that the master showman, Florenz Ziegfeld, starred him in the Ziegfeld Follies for the next ten years.

THE COLORED ORPHAN ASYLUM

The Colored Orphan Asylum took up the entire west side of Fifth Avenue between 44th and 45th Streets.

*This was the quiet scene near Grand Central Station
(the small building at right) in 1853. The Colored Orphan
Asylum, which stood at Fifth Avenue and 44th Street, is
the large building to the left.*

Organized in 1836 by two white women, Mrs. Anna
Shotwell and her niece, the institution moved from its
original location at 12th Street when the city donated
the Fifth Avenue land. During the height of the Civil
War draft riots in 1863, a mob burned the asylum to the
ground. Only quick thinking by the staff, most of whom
were white, saved all the children from harm. The
orphanage Bible, rescued by an eight-year-old girl, was
the only thing salvaged from the flames. The work of
Mrs. Shotwell and her niece is carried on today by the
Riverdale Children's Association of New York.

PART SIX

RADIO CITY

RADIO CITY, or Rockefeller Center as it is also called, is an area of towering skyscrapers today. Radio City Music Hall is here, and so is the famous mall with its skating rink in the winter and its patio for outdoor dining in the summer. Many radio and television shows originate here, and there are different restaurants and shops where one can buy all kinds of items from different parts of the world.

NEGROES MOVE NORTH

The Rockefeller Center area was once the heart of the middle-class Negro population in New York. Mount Olivet Baptist Church, St. Mark's Methodist Church and St. Benedict the Moor Roman Catholic Church were only three of the many houses of worship that had followed their congregations northward in the city. There were several hotels owned by Negroes in the area, too. The Marshal Hotel had a cabaret that was very popular with both Negroes and white people who were prominent in the theatrical and sports worlds. A frequent visitor to the cabaret was Isaac Murphy, a Negro, who was the first jockey to ride three Kentucky Derby winners.

There was also an exclusive club here called the Sons of New York. Lewis Latimer, the well-known member of the Edison Pioneers, lived at 324 West 55th Street in 1890. Another Negro inventor, Granville Woods, lived close to the present site of Radio City.

HOTEL MACEO

The Hotel Maceo, at 213 West 53rd Street, was Negro owned and operated. A banquet was held there in 1900 to honor Congressman George H. White of North Carolina. He was the last of the Negroes elected to Congress during the Reconstruction. In his speech at the banquet, Congressman White said, in part:

> This is the Negro's farewell to the American Congress, but let me say that Phoenix-like he will rise up some day and come again. These parting words are in behalf of an outraged, heartbroken, bruised and bleeding but God-fearing people; faithful, industrious, rising people —full of potential force.

W. C. HANDY MUSIC PUBLISHING COMPANY

W. C. Handy, known as the "Father of the Blues," owned a music publishing company at 1650 Broadway

W. C. Handy as a youth, long before he became famous as the "Father of the Blues."

(at the corner of 51st Street). This concern has been in continuous operation since 1917. Handy was the composer of "The St. Louis Blues" and many other popular songs, some of which have become modern classics. When he first came to New York from Chicago (he was originally from Memphis, Tennessee), he had difficulty renting an office in the Rialto Building on "Music Row," an area devoted to music companies. In the beginning, a white lawyer shared his office with Handy. The firm became so successful that eventually the lawyer turned the entire office over to Handy. The Handy Music Publishing Company is now managed by Handy's son and daughters.

THE NATIONAL URBAN LEAGUE

The home of the National Urban League is at 55 East 52nd Street. Organized in 1910, this interracial endeavor now has branches in thirty-three states. It is concerned with the improvement of social and economic conditions among Negroes.

THE NATIONAL ASSOCIATION FOR THE ADVANCEMENT OF COLORED PEOPLE

The National Association for the Advancement of Colored People, at 1790 Broadway, was organized in 1909. This interracial group, especially its famous Legal Defense Fund, works through legal procedures to assert the claims of American Negroes to first-class, unqualified citizenship. A past president of the NAACP, Arthur B. Spingarn, prepares an annual bibliography of publications by and about Negroes. The Legal Rights Association, a forerunner of today's NAACP, worked for civil rights for Negroes as early as 1858.

CATO'S LANE

There used to be a short street at Third Avenue and 52nd Street called Cato's Lane. It was famous for a roadhouse operated by a Negro named Cato Alexander. The roadhouse was frequented by socialites who used Cato's Lane as a route to the open countryside. Cato Alexander and his roadhouse were well known throughout the city.

CARNEGIE HALL

Carnegie Hall, at Seventh Avenue and 57th Street, is New York's oldest concert auditorium. It has been the scene of many musical triumphs for both Negroes and white people. History was made there in 1912 when New York's first jazz concert was held. James Reese Europe and his Clef Club were the performers. One hundred twenty-five musicians, including ten pianists, performed on that occasion. James Europe and his musicians received rave reviws. The Clef Club, an organization of Negro musicians, had a clubhouse on the present site of the Donnell Library, at 20 West 53rd Street.

Carnegie Hall was also the scene of a mass meeting held in 1900 by the Citizens Protective League to protest the attitudes revealed by the police during the 1900 riots. This was the first time New York Negroes demanded impartial treatment from the police.

MARY McLEOD BETHUNE

The late Mary McLeod Bethune organized the National Council of Negro Women, composed of affiliated groups of women's clubs in cities and towns all across the country. Its present offices are at 145 West 52nd Street. Mrs. Bethune founded the Bethune-Cookman College in Florida, and during Franklin D. Roosevelt's administration, she was an advisor to the Government on matters concerning young people. Her favorite advice to the young was to "know where you've been and you'll know where you're going."

THE COLORED HOME AND HOSPITAL

First Avenue and 65th Street was the site of the Colored Home and Hospital. It consisted of a hospital, a chapel and a home for the aged.

NEGRO EXPLORERS

The Explorers Club, at 40 East 70th Street, is a private organization composed of famous explorers. One of its members was the late Matthew Henson, a Negro explorer who accompanied Admiral Peary on all of his trips to the Arctic. Henson actually planted the American flag at the North Pole.

Of course, Negroes have been explorers since the distant past. Upon his return from the New World, Columbus reported that natives had told him they traded with and obtained gold from black men who sailed from the south and southeast. Two-thousand-year-old stone figures with Negroid features have been found in Mexico, and early Spanish and Portuguese explorers were accompanied by Negroes. In 1859, a Negro exploring party set out from New York City and sailed across the Atlantic to explore the Niger Valley in Africa. The party was directed by Martin Delany, a Harvard-educated physician.

Doctor Delaney was a brilliant man with a fierce pride in being black. With Frederick Douglass, he was co-founder of the newspaper the *North Star*. Douglass once said of Delany, "While I thank God for simply making me a man, Delany thanks God for making him a black man." Delany was the author of *The Condition, Elevation, Emigration and Destiny of the Colored People of the United States, Politically Considered*, which was published in 1852. He described American Negroes as "a nation within a nation" and yearned for a country where Negroes could command respect. This led him to persuade three Negro merchants to finance the purchase of a ship, the *Mendi*, which was named for an African

Major Martin R. Delany, Harvard-educated physician and explorer of the Niger Valley in Africa.

tribe. Delany and his companions explored the Niger Valley in September, 1859. He made a treaty with chiefs of the Egba tribe for land to be colonized by American Negroes. Upon his return to the United States, however, the Civil War broke out and his plans had to be put aside. Delany was a major in the Union Army, charged with the recruitment of Negro troops. After the war, Delany retired to private medical practice in Xenia, Ohio, where he died in 1885.

PART SEVEN

CENTRAL PARK

NEW YORK'S "back yard" is the affectionate term for this touch of country in the middle of Manhattan. Stretching from 59th to 110th Streets and from Fifth Avenue to Central Park West, it has become a playground for young and old alike. Open-air concerts are held in the park every summer, and whether one prefers Bach or the Beatles, there is music to suit every taste. Shakespeare, too, has his followers, and many a New York youngster first met Macbeth in Central Park. In the winter, skaters and sledders enjoy Central Park in the snow.

The park was laid out by Frederick Law Olmsted, a famous landscape designer and architect. He also designed Morningside Park in upper Manhattan, Prospect Park in Brooklyn, and countless other parks all over America.

Olmsted hated slavery. He spent several months traveling through the slave states trying to convince slave owners that slavery was degrading to the owners as well as dehumanizing to the slaves. He also argued that slavery was economically unsound. Out of his experience, Olmsted wrote *A Journey in the Seaboard Slave States*, a classic essay of the slave period, and two other books, *A Journey Through Texas* and *A Journey in the Back Country*. All three books were condensed in *The Cotton Kingdom*, published in 1861.

After he started designing Central Park, Olmsted temporarily put it aside to work for the Union cause in the Civil War. After the war, he was associated with the Freedmen's Bureau, helping Negroes to adjust to the new conditions. Finally, he returned to New York to finish his work on Central Park.

SAN JUAN HILL

The area around Amsterdam Avenue and 63rd Street was named for a bloody battle of the Spanish-American War. On San Juan Hill in New York, Negroes and immigrants fought for living space and jobs. Negroes also felt that they were fighting to maintain their dignity and self-respect. If a place and a year had to be selected to pinpoint when "new" citizens (white immigrants) began to consider "old" New Yorkers (Negroes) as neighborhood intruders, it would have to be San Juan Hill about 1910.

Mary White Ovington, a white woman who had been both a social worker and a journalist, came to live in San Juan Hill. She wanted to know how she could best help the Negroes who lived there to improve their conditions. William Lewis Bulkley, a former slave who had worked hard to earn a Ph.D. degree from Syracuse University, also moved into the area. He was a public school teacher and eventually became a principal. In San Juan Hill, he started a night school for adults and a kindergarten for the children of working mothers. The Hope Day Nursery took care of the preschool children.

Miss Ovington persuaded wealthy people to invest in modern housing in the area. The Tuskegee Apartments were built in 1909 on West 62nd Street, followed by the Hampton Apartments around the corner a year later. Both Bulkley and Miss Ovington were among the founders of the NAACP and the National Urban League.

One of the residents of San Juan Hill was Dr. Rogers W. Griffin, a Negro podiatrist who had his practice in the same house on West 62nd Street from 1919 to 1959.

Much of this area is now part of Lincoln Center for the Performing Arts, where many Negroes perform regularly. Leontyne Price, the renowned Negro soprano, starred in the first performance of the Metropolitan Opera Company in its new quarters in Lincoln Center.

THE NEW-YORK HISTORICAL SOCIETY

The length of Eighth Avenue that forms the western boundary of Central Park is called Central Park West. The New-York Historical Society is located on Central

Park West at 77th Street. In addition to miniature paintings of Pierre Toussaint, there are facsimiles of letters written by Benjamin Banneker, a Negro who made the first clock in America in 1753 from parts made by him in this country. Before that, clock parts and whole clocks had to be imported from England. Banneker also wrote almanacs and helped to lay out the nation's Capitol. The New-York Historical Society also has many other items and manuscripts that connect Negroes with the history of New York.

THE ELDORADO APARTMENTS

The block from 90th Street to 91st Street on Central Park West is taken up by the twin-tower Eldorado apartment building. At one time, it was merely one small item in the real estate empire built on nickel and dime collections taken up by the late Daddy Grace, a Negro evangelist.

THE MUSEUM OF THE CITY OF NEW YORK

The Museum of the City of New York, at Fifth Avenue and 103rd Street, unveiled a bust of Eubie Blake in 1967. Blake is a Negro composer and pianist. With Noble Sissle, he formed one of the immortal teams in American show business. Although it displays three hundred years of history, this museum contains surprisingly little that pertains to the Negro.

*Eubie Blake on the occasion of the presentation of his bust
to the Theatre and Music Collection of the Museum of
the City of New York.*

PART EIGHT

HARLEM

MOST people think that Harlem consists entirely of antiquated tenements that are practically unfit for human habitation. While it is true that too many of the buildings fit that description, there are others that would be an asset to any neighborhood. Even thirty years ago sections of Harlem were positively swank. In the past ten to fifteen years there has been a tremendous number of new housing units built by both public and private agencies. One of the oddities of New York City is that few areas remain unchanged for any length of time; this is as true of Harlem as it is of Greenwich Village, Washington Heights or any other section.

FREDERICK DOUGLASS CIRCLE

Where Central Park West again becomes Eighth Avenue at 110th Street, Harlem begins. Frederick Douglass Circle is located at this junction. Douglass was a former slave whose biography reveals why he was one of the great Americans of all time. In addition to his

This signpost at West 110th Street honors a great American. It is ironic that Douglass' name is misspelled on the sign.

other accomplishments, Douglass established the *North Star,* an abolitionist newspaper which he edited for seventeen years.

In 1872, Douglass was a candidate for the Vice-Presidency of the United States on the Equal Women's Rights ticket. Victoria C. Woodhull was the party's choice for President. Most people think only of Negroes when equal rights are mentioned. Douglass and Sojourner Truth saw women's rights and civil rights simply as a part of the whole struggle to win human rights for all Americans.

Douglass' *Life and Times of Frederick Douglass* was published in 1882. In it he describes the difficulties he had as a fugitive slave in New York, where even Negroes would turn him in for a few dollars. He also wrote of the kindness and help given to him by strangers, both Negro and white. He died in 1895.

A. PHILIP RANDOLPH SQUARE

Where Seventh Avenue and St. Nicholas Avenue come together at 117th Street is A. Philip Randolph Square. Randolph has devoted his life to the improvement of economic and social conditions for all people. He was instrumental in organizing the Brotherhood of Sleeping Car Porters against almost overwhelming odds. This victory restored the dignity of Negro railroad porters, who had been forced to depend upon tips for a living. Randolph is currently an international vice-president of the American Federation of Labor–Congress of Industrial Organizations.

In 1941, almost single-handedly, he persuaded President Franklin D. Roosevelt to set up the Fair Employment Practices Commission. This made it possible for Negroes to work in defense jobs which had previously been barred to them despite the war that was going on.

MORNINGSIDE PARK

This hilly park is west of Randolph Square. Crossing the park to Morningside Heights beyond, one follows the footsteps of Revolutionary War soldiers. One can also see the Morningside Gardens Apartments. This is an integrated community of people from almost every nation on earth.

CARL SCHURZ MEMORIAL

At Morningside Drive and 116th Street there is a statue of Carl Schurz. On the base of the statue are scenes showing his activities on behalf of Negroes and Indians. Schurz had to flee from his native Germany because of his revolutionary activities. He arrived in the United States in 1852 and was soon involved in politics. He helped to organize the Republican party. In addition to being an editor and author, he was a diplomat and a United States Senator.

COLUMBIA UNIVERSITY

West of Morningside Park stands Columbia University and many other cultural and educational institutions. The Columbia University library contains the Gumby Collection of newspaper clippings, which was assembled by a Negro. It also has a copy of "The Principia" prepared by the New York City Suffrage Committee of Colored Citizens in 1860, a copy of the minutes of the New York State Convention of Colored Men held in 1854, and other items of interest to the student of Negro history.

Columbia Presbyterian Hospital, which is further north in Washington Heights, was built with funds donated by Robert Lenox and other philanthropists. Lenox donated money on one condition: there must be a plaque in the building indicating that the hospital was dedicated to serving the medical needs of the poor of New York City, regardless of their race, color or creed.

RICHARD T. GREENER

Grant's Tomb is at Riverside Drive and 122nd Street. The secretary of the commission which set up the tomb was Richard T. Greener, a native of Philadelphia and the first Negro to graduate from Harvard University. From 1873 to 1877, he was professor of Greek, Latin, constitutional law and international law at the University of South Carolina. While there, Greener served on the commission that set up the public school system for all the children of South Carolina.

When the Ku Klux Klan spirit and the Black Code took control in the South in 1877, Greener's career in Carolina ended. He accepted a position as Dean of Howard University's Law School. For a while, in 1885, he served as a New York City Civil Service Examiner. Then he entered the United States Foreign Service, from which he retired in 1905. Greener died in Chicago in 1922.

UPTOWN MUSEUMS

There is an interesting group of buildings on Broadway between 156th and 157th Streets. One is the Museum of the American Indian; another is the Hispanic Museum. The Numismatic Society and the Geographic Society complete the group. The Numismatic Society has a collection of anti-slavery coins, medals and tokens of interest to the student of Negro history. At Broadway and 156th Street, across from the museums, is Trinity Graveyard, where many famous people are buried, including Clement Clarke Moore, John Jacob Astor and James Audubon.

JUMEL MANSION

The Jumel Mansion, a landmark of the Revolutionary War period at Edgecombe Avenue and 160th Street, is open to the public. Madame Jumel was a widow who married Aaron Burr. It seems that Burr, who was not an admirable man according to history, was frequently in need of money. He borrowed from George de Grasse, putting up a deed for some property on Varick Street as collateral. Burr never repaid the loan, and George T. Downing, who married a daughter of de Grasse's, eventually came into possession of the deed.

PRINCE HALL

A Negro veteran of the Revolutionary War, Prince Hall, formed a Masonic lodge in 1787 in Boston after obtaining a charter from London. The branch of the Masonic Order located at 454 West 155th Street in New York is named in honor of Prince Hall. He petitioned the Massachusetts legislature to stop the slave trade and to establish schools for Negro children.

HAMILTON GRANGE

In 1801 Alexander Hamilton built a country house, Hamilton Grange, now at 287 Convent Avenue. It now belongs to the Federal Government, but it is in a sad state of repair. It was at one time the rectory of St. Luke's Church, which is next door.

STRIVERS ROW

The houses on 138th and 139th Streets, between Seventh and Eighth Avenues, have been called Strivers

*These West 139th Street houses on "Strivers Row"
represent nineteenth century elegance. They were
designed by Stanford White.*

Row. They were built between 1889 and 1891 as suburban homes for wealthy people who wished to live "in the country." Lack of public transportation caused the plan to fall through, and the houses were sold to Negroes, who had moved to Harlem in great numbers by then.

The houses were designed by Stanford White, the well-known architect. They are elegant, and they have such exterior features as courtyards and driveways. Harlem residents referred to the people who bought these homes as "folks striving to get up in the world"—hence the name Strivers Row. New York City has designated this area as a landmark which is to be preserved intact.

THE BLACK SWAN RECORD COMPANY

The basement of 257 West 138th Street housed the first office and factory of the Black Swan Record Company, the first such firm owned and operated by Negroes. One of the company's early recording artists was Ethel Waters. The company sold a half million records during its first six months. As it expanded, the company moved to larger quarters at 2289 Seventh Avenue. Black Swan records are now collectors' items.

DORRANCE BROOKS SQUARE

The intersection of 137th Street and St. Nicholas Avenue was renamed Dorrance Brooks Square in honor

of a Negro hero of World War I who was a member of
the 369th Regiment.

THE WHITE ROSE MISSION

The White Rose Mission, at 262 West 137th Street, is
a haven for working girls. It was established in 1897 by
Mrs. Victoria Earle Matthews, a former slave. She
learned from experience how difficult it was for Negro
girls from the South to find nice homes in the North. It
was Mrs. Matthews' custom to meet trains and boats and
offer assistance to the young Negro girls she saw. Mrs.
Matthews opened her home to these girls and watched
over them until they were more able to care for themselves. She was the national organizer for the National
Council of Colored Women, the first group of its kind
in the United States.

THE HOPE DAY NURSERY

The Hope Day Nursery, at 2112 Madison Avenue, is
another pioneer social agency set up by Negroes to help
themselves. Founded in 1902, it is still in existence.

"PIG FOOT MARY"

The southwest corner of Seventh Avenue and 137th
Street was once the property of "Pig Foot Mary," a poor,

illiterate Negro woman who peddled soul food on the
streets of Harlem. Her real name was Mrs. Lillian Dean
Harris, and although she was penniless when she arrived
in New York from Mississippi, she invested in real estate
with the money she earned as a peddler. Eventually, she
retired to a life of relative ease in California.

ABYSSINIAN BAPTIST CHURCH

The present site of the Abyssinian Baptist Church is
138 West 138th Street. It was founded in 1808 on Worth
Street in lower Manhattan. It moved north gradually,
following the movement of the congregation.

Marcus Garvey's Liberty Hall adjoined the church's
present site. Today Liberty Hall is an apartment building. Garvey started the Universal Negro Improvement
Association in 1917. His theme was pride in black skin
and economic independence. His followers elected him
Provisional President of Africa. The U.N.I.A. was the
first nationwide "black nationalist" organization of this
century.

MOTHER AFRICAN METHODIST
EPISCOPAL ZION CHURCH

The pioneer of all Negro churches in the city is Mother
A.M.E. Zion at 146 West 137th Street. This is the present
location of the church that started at 156 Church Street

*The 1808 original site of the Abyssinian Church was at
40 Worth Street. It is now located at 138 West 138th Street.*

in 1796. It has been in continuous existence since that time. Many notable events have taken place within the walls of its various homes. In 1829, a woman known simply as Isabella stood up in the middle of a service and renounced her name and said that henceforth she would be known as Sojourner Truth. "Sojourner," she explained, "because I am a wanderer, Truth because God is Truth so Truth shall be my my abiding name until I die."

The funeral of the Negro actress Florence Mills in 1927 was probably the most moving event that has taken place at Mother Zion. Almost everyone in Harlem tried to attend the funeral or watch the procession pass. As the hearse went up Seventh Avenue, a flock of blackbirds was released from an airplane overhead.

SMALLS PARADISE

In 1925, Edwin Smalls and his brother, Charles, moved their famous Fifth Avenue cabaret to 2294 Seventh Avenue. The club is now known as Big Wilt's Smalls Paradise. From 1925 to the early 1940's, Smalls Paradise was the king of a group of Harlem nightclubs that attracted people from all over the city.

DR. GODFREY NURSE

One of New York City's few Negro millionaires, Dr. Godfrey Nurse, lives at 186 West 135th Street. He is well

SMALLS

CAFETERIA

The place where the joy
makers abide. Whistle a
bit, Dance a bit, laugh
all the time.

Edwin Smalls, Prop.

Maybell Smith
Mildred Brown

2212 Fifth Avenue

Bet. 134th & 135th St.

*An advertisement for Smalls Cafeteria which appeared
in a 1923 magazine.*

known for his gift of $100,000 to Harlem Hospital, which
established a series of lectures for medical students that
will enable them to improve the health of the people in
Harlem.

ST. PHILIP'S CHURCH

St. Philip's Church, at 213 West 134th Street, was
organized in 1809, but it wasn't until 1816 that the first
church was built in the Centre Street area. At one time,
St. Philip's owned one entire block of houses in Harlem.

THE LAFAYETTE THEATER

The proving ground for Negro stage performers, the
Lafayette Theater, was on Seventh Avenue between
131st and 132nd Streets. In 1913, Leubrie Hill produced
the "Darktown Follies" there and revolutionized the
standards for musical revues. Florenz Ziegfeld, the master showman, bought a portion of Hill's show and incorporated it into the Ziegfeld Follies.

THE AMSTERDAM NEWS

The business office of Harlem's weekly newspaper,
the *Amsterdam News,* is at 2340 Eighth Avenue. The
paper is owned and controlled by Negroes.

HOTEL THERESA

The most famous hotel in Harlem is the Hotel Theresa at Seventh Avenue and 125th Street. It is now a landmark, and is being converted into an office building to be named in honor of Dr. Martin Luther King, Jr. When Fidel Castro came to speak at the United Nations, he stayed at the Theresa, where he met with Premier Khrushchev of the Soviet Union.

BLUMSTEIN'S DEPARTMENT STORE

Another Harlem landmark, Blumstein's Department Store, at 230 West 125th Street, is the place where Dr. King was stabbed by a deranged Negro woman some years ago.

CARVER SAVINGS AND LOAN

The first Negro-owned and -operated bank in New York State, Carver Savings and Loan, is at 75 West 125th Street. It was started in 1948 and now has two branches, one on 23rd Street and the other in Brooklyn.

THE NATIONAL MEMORIAL BOOK STORE

The National Memorial Book Store was opposite the Hotel Theresa at 2107 Seventh Avenue. It was on the

site of the new state office building, and is now temporarily located at 101 West 125th Street. It will move into
permanent quarters in the New York State Office Building when that structure is completed. The store special-
izes in black nationalist literature as well as in contemporary books by or about Negroes. The rear section of the
old store held a small exhibit of rare photographs of important Negroes. Occasionally, art shows were held at
the store. The sidewalk in front of the National Memorial
Book Store was a popular site for soap-box orators to
expound their various philosophies.

ETHIOPIAN HEBREW CONGREGATION

The Ethiopian Hebrew Congregation's synagogue,
1 West 123rd Street, is just off Mount Morris Park. New
York City has had a congregation of black Jews since
1845. There have been black Jews for thousands of
years, particularly in Ethiopia, where they are known
as Falashas (members of the Hamitic tribe).

The Mount Morris Park firetower is a relic from the
days when volunteer firemen had to keep watch for fires.
That hill was the scene of skirmishes during the Revolutionary War.

LANGSTON HUGHES

The beloved Negro poet Langston Hughes lived at
20 East 127th Street. He died in 1967.

House of worship for black Jews of Harlem
at 1 West 123rd Street.

FATHER DIVINE

The last "heaven" in Harlem of the late Negro evangelist, Father Divine, is at 13-17 West 128th Street. During the Depression of the 1930's, there were many such lodgings in the city, and others were scattered throughout the United States.

ASTOR ROW

The south side of 130th Street between Lenox and Fifth Avenues is known as Astor Row. The houses were built by John J. Astor when he was the biggest landlord in the city. This street still maintains an air of genteel respectability.

THE NEW AMSTERDAM MUSICAL ASSOCIATION

The clubhouse of the New Amsterdam Musical Association is at 107 West 130th Street. Organized in 1905, this group broke through the color barrier in the musicians union. It is still in existence.

COUNTEE CULLEN LIBRARY

Countee Cullen Library, named for a well-known poet and schoolteacher, is at 104 West 136th Street. An elaborate town house once stood on this site. It was built by

The last Harlem "heaven" is located at
13-17 West 128th Street.

Mme. C. J. Walker, who manufactured and sold beauty products. She became a very wealthy woman. Her daughter Aleila set aside a floor in the $90,000 mansion for the use of struggling writers and artists. This generous action helped to produce the renaissance in Negro art and literature during the 1920's and 1930's.

HARLEM HOSPITAL

Harlem Hospital's new addition at Lenox Avenue and 136th Street may be seen by walking to Lenox Avenue from the Cullen Library. It was 1919 before Negro doctors and nurses were added to the staff of this hospital, which serves the Negro community.

THE SAVOY BALLROOM

The "Home of Happy Feet," the Savoy Ballroom, was once at Lenox Avenue and 141st Street. The Lindy Hop and other dance fads started at the Savoy. And it was here that a shy and sometimes awkward girl began her long trek to the top of the entertainment world. Today she is the acknowledged queen of song, Ella Fitzgerald.

THE SCHOMBURG COLLECTION

The Schomburg Collection on the Negro is housed at 103 West 135th Street. Arthur Schomburg was a Puerto Rican of modest means who devoted his time to collecting rare and valuable works by and about the Negro. New York City purchased his collection and has used it as a base for the finest collection of reference works by and about the Negro in this part of the country. It is administered by the New York Public Library, and it compares favorably with any collection of its kind in the United States.

The basement of the building was once a center for little theater groups. One such group was the Krigwa Players. In a handbill distributed in 1920, the Krigwa Players described their objectives in these words:

> An attempt to establish in High Harlem, New York City, a little theater which shall be primarily a center where Negro actors, before Negro audiences, interpret Negro life as depicted by Negro artists; but which shall always have a welcome for all artists of all races and for all sympathetic comers and for all beautiful ideas.

In the library basement, one can see the strikingly beautiful murals created by the famous artist Aaron Douglas when he was a young man.

History is made by people—the place where history is made is only incidental. Yet who can deny that there is something special about Manhattan? It has lured people to its shores for centuries. Now, as one strolls about the city, one can be directly and visually aware of the connection between the Negro and the history of New York. What is true of New York is true of most American towns and cities; it is simply impossible to separate the history of America from the history of the Negro in America.

SUGGESTED READINGS

Guidebooks to Supplement the Negro History Tour

Jewish Welfare Board, *The Book of Trips to Places of Jewish Interest*. New York: Jewish Welfare Board, 1939.

Koeuwenhoven, John A., ed., *The New York Guidebook*. New York: Dell Publishing Co., 1964.

Simon, Kate, *New York Places and Pleasures*. Cleveland: Meridian Books, 1959.

Formal and Informal Histories

Botkin, B. A., *New York City Folklore*. New York: Random House, 1956. Contains interesting anecdotes.

Hughes, Langston, and Meltzer, Milton, *Black Magic: A Pictorial History of the Negro in American Entertainment*. Englewood Cliffs, N.J.: Prentice-Hall, 1967.

Johnson, James Weldon, *Black Manhattan*. New York: Alfred A. Knopf, 1930.

O'Callaghan, W., ed., *Colonial History of the State of New York*. Albany, N.Y.: Weed and Parsons, 1854; Vol. III, pp. 614-615, and Vol. IV, pp. 510-511.

Osofsky, Gilbert, *Harlem: The Making of a Ghetto*. New York: Harper & Row, 1963. Traces the history of New York's Negro population in the nineteenth and twentieth centuries. Especially valuable for its notes and bibliography.

Ottley, Roi, and Weatherby, William J., eds., *The Negro in New York*. New York: New York Public Library, 1967. A compilation of research papers by the Works Progress Administration.

Ovington, Mary White, *Half a Man: The Status of the Negro in New York*. London: Longmans, Green and Co., 1911.

Stokes, I. N. Phelps, *The Iconography of Manhattan Island, 1498-1909*. New York: R. H. Dodd, 1918, 6 vols. Gives details of land grants and other information of value to students of Negro History in Volumes IV and VI.

Diaries and Recollections

Dunaway, Philip, and Evans, Mel, eds., *A Treasury of the World's Great Diaries*. Garden City, N.Y.: Doubleday & Company, 1957. Mayor Philip Hone describes his connection with Thomas Downing (p. 548).

Dunlap, William, *Memoirs of a Water Drinker*. New York: Saunders and Otley, 1837. Chapter 14 is devoted to Cato Alexander and his famous tavern.